YOUR KNOWLEDGE HAS VALUE

An Introduction to Blockchain and AI in Food Supply Chain in Smart Cities. Reducing Waste

Somdip Dey

Bibliographic information published by the German National Library:

The German National Library lists this publication in the National Bibliography; detailed bibliographic data are available on the Internet at http://dnb.dnb.de.

ISBN: 9783346678010
This book is also available as an ebook.

Coverbild: Sashkin @shutterstock.com

© GRIN Publishing GmbH
Nymphenburger Straße 86
80636 München

Print and binding: Books on Demand GmbH, Norderstedt, Germany
Printed on acid-free paper from responsible sources.

The present work has been carefully prepared. Nevertheless, authors and publishers do not incur liability for the correctness of information, notes, links and advice as well as any printing errors.

GRIN web shop: https://www.grin.com/document/1194960

An Introduction to Blockchain and AI in Food Supply Chain in Smart Cities: Reducing Waste

Somdip Dey

Nosh Technologies & University of Essex

About the author

Somdip Dey

Somdip Dey FRSA, also professionally known as InteliDey, is an Indian-born embedded machine learning researcher, educator, entrepreneur and electronic music producer. Dey is widely credited to co-develop the Nosh app, which is an artificial intelligence powered food management application, aiming to reduce food waste in the household. He is also the co-founder and CEO of Nosh Technologies, which is a deep tech company, developing cutting edge technologies to reduce food waste and improve sustainability of the planet. Dey is named a Fellow of the Royal Society of Arts, an MIT Innovator Under 35 Europe and a World IP Review Leader for his contributions in developing embedded machine learning technologies to reduce food waste and help the society.

Website

https://books.noshdaily.com

This book is accompanied by the above website. The website provides a variety of supplementary material, including exercises, lecture slides, corrections of mistakes, and other resources that should be useful to both readers and instructors.

Acknowledgements

I would like to take this opportunity to extend my thanks to many people who directly and indirectly supported me to improve this book. First of all, I would like to thank my parents - Sudip Dey and Soma Dey, without whom I might never have found my passion to help others using technology. Next, it goes without saying that how lucky I have been to be supervised by Dr. Amit Kumar Singh and Prof. Klaus Dieter McDonald-Maier, who have always supported me and have given me the full freedom to pursue my research during my PhD. I couldn't have asked for any better to be my mentor and advisor during my PhD journey than Dr. Amit Kumar Singh and Prof. Klaus Dieter McDonald-Maier.

Many thanks also to everyone in the Embedded and Intelligent Systems Laboratory at the University of Essex for their continued support, advise and friendship. I would also like to thank Suman Saha, Chief Technology Officer of Nosh Technologies, for his support to build one of the most successful food management and waste reduction startups in the world. Also, without Suman's support this research work would not have been possible.

Abstract

Food waste is an important social and environmental issue that the current society faces, where one third of the total food produced is wasted or lost every year while more than 820 million people around the world do not have access to adequate food. However, as we move towards a decentralized Web 3.0 enabled smart city, we can utilize cutting edge technologies such as blockchain, artificial intelligence, cloud computing and many more to reduce food waste in different phases of the supply chain. In this book, we introduce FoodSQRBlock and SmartNoshWaste - two blockchain based multi-layered frameworks in the food supply chain utilizing cloud computing, QR code and reinforcement learning to reduce food waste.

Contents

1 **Preface**   **1**

2 **Introduction**   **2**

3 **Prerequisite: Blockchain, AI, QR Code and Cloud Computing**   **7**

       3.0.1   Blockchain Technology 7

       3.0.2   AI and Reinforcement Learning 8

       3.0.3   QR Code 8

       3.0.4   Cloud Computing 9

4 **FoodSQRBlock: FoodSQRBlock: Digitizing Food Production and the Supply Chain Data**   **11**

     4.1   Proposed Framework: FoodSQRBlock 11

     4.2   Experimental evaluation: case study & large scale integration of FoodSQRBlock 15

       4.2.1   Experimental Evaluation 15

       4.2.2   Analysis & Discussion 16

     4.3   Future Direction and Discussion 16

     4.4   Summary 16

5 **SmartNoshWaste: Using Blockchain & Machine Learning in Food Supply Chain to Reduce Waste**   **17**

     5.1   Proposed Framework: SmartNoshWaste 17

       5.1.1   Assumptions and data system architecture of SmartNoshWaste 17

       5.1.2   Machine learning module of SmartNoshWaste 21

     5.2   Experimental evaluation: Case study with real food data 22

     5.3   Future Direction and Discussion 24

     5.4   Summary 25

Bibliography   **26**

List of Figures

2.1 Representational diagram of a smart city using technologies such as Blockchain, Artificial Intelligence (A.I.), Cloud and Edge Computing and many more within the Web 3.0 information system 2

2.2 UPC barcode for Tropicana Trop50 Blackberry Cherry juice as fetched from BarcodeSpider.com [bar, b] 4

3.1 Representative diagram of intelligent agent 9

3.2 Representational QR code with "Hello, World!" message embedding 9

4.1 Overview of the System Architecture of FoodSQRBlock based on Farm-to-Fork supply chain 12

4.2 Conceptual FoodSQRBlock framework of an agri-food supply chain traceability system based on QR code & blockchain technology 13

4.3 QR code holding information of a dairy product, which is produced at Boydells Dairy Farm in the UK, generated by FoodSQRBlock 14

4.4 Time taken to process different number of items (using FoodSQRBlock) in Google Cloud Platform's Compute Engine 15

5.1 Overview of the Data System Architecture of SmartNoshWaste based on Farm-to-Fork supply chain 18

5.2 Generic data regarding food in different phases of the supply chain that are digitized to be stored in the blockchain 19

5.3 Diagramatic representation of Q-Learning based RL method in the Machine Learning Module of SmartNoshWaste 21

5.4 Consumption and wastage data on potatoes collected via the nosh app [nos,] where the Y-Axis represents the number of items consumed ($'C$) or wasted (W) and X-Axis represents the months of the year when the data was collected 23

Chapter 1

Preface

Before I introduce the works on how Blockchain and Artificial Intelligence (AI) are being used in the food supply chain, please allow me to share my story. In 2013, I moved to the U.K. to pursue my master's degree in Advanced Computer Science at the University of Manchester. In 2014, while completing my master's degree, my parents in India went through a tragic car accident that caused severe injuries to my mother and paralyzed my father. To help my parents go through medical procedures, I sent back all my money to them in India without realizing that I didn't have any money to buy food for almost a week. To survive from hunger I ended up salvaging edibles from dustbins on the streets of Manchester. Don't worry, the collected foods were completely edible but were thrown away by others because either of inconvenience or the food were one day past their "best-before" date. This showed me, how much food wastage happens yet we have so many hungry people around the world.

Later in 2014, after graduating with my master's degree with a specialization in Computer Systems Engineering, I co-developed the world's first crowd food-sharing platform that enables users to share their leftovers and food surplus with other people-in-need nearby. This application also won the 3Scale API award at the 2014 Koding's Global Virtual Hackathon and in the following years, it also inspired many other entrepreneurs to join the fight against food waste by developing similar solutions.

Being an early adopter and creator of such a technology that helped build the personal food waste management industry, I have been closely following food waste and related statistics around the world. As the human population grew over the years, food waste also scaled up accordingly. According to the U.S. Food and Agriculture Organization (FAO), more than 1.3 billion tons of food are wasted around the globe, which is worth $2.6 trillion. On the other hand, we have more than 820 million people around the globe who do not have access to proper nutrition. That being said, food wastage is not a social issue but an environmental one as well. Food wastage also contributes to almost 10% of global carbon emissions. Food waste is an issue that is currently plaguing the world and it happens throughout the food supply chain regardless.

Being a technologist and a scientist in the field of AI and Blockchain, I strongly believe that we can use such technologies to reduce waste, improve efficiency and improve sustainability in the food supply chain. So, without further ado let's get started!

Chapter 2

Introduction

Smart cities are often visualized as consortium of technologies including sensors, computing systems and services, across many scales that are connected through multiple networks which provide continuous data regarding the activities of people and objects including devices, buildings and assets in terms of the flow of decisions about the physical, operational and social form of the city [Batty et al., 2012]. On the other hand, as we move towards Web 3.0 with focus on decentralized semantic web [Alabdulwahhab, 2018, Ragnedda and Destefanis, 2019], it is unavoidable to imagine smart cities of the future without decentralized Web 3.0 as the underlying information system.

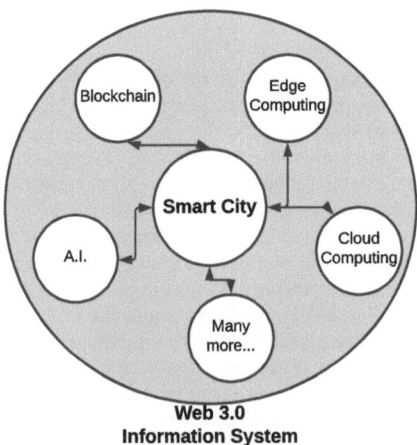

Figure 2.1: Representational diagram of a smart city using technologies such as Blockchain, Artificial Intelligence (A.I.), Cloud and Edge Computing and many more within the Web 3.0 information system

Fig. 2.1 shows the diagrammatic representation of a smart city utilizing Web 3.0 information system along with other technologies such as Blockchain, Artificial Intelligence (A.I. or simply, AI) Cloud Computing, Edge Computing and many more, to feed information from each other to optimize the efficiency of city operations and services and connect to the citizens [Peris-Ortiz et al., 2017]. The key goals of information flow within the smart cities could include a plethora of activities including managing traffic and transportation systems, power plants, utilities, water supply networks, waste, crime detection, information systems, schools, libraries, hospitals, and other community services.

On the other hand, one of the most important issues that the modern society faces today is food wastage, which is both a social issue and an environmental one [Schanes et al., 2018, foo, a, foo, b]. Every year one third of total food produced, which weighs approximately 1.3 billion tonnes and is equivalent to $2.6 trillion, is lost or wasted. However, more than 820 million people around the globe doesn't have access to proper nutritious meal [foo, a]. Moreover, food waste and loss contributes to almost 10% of the total greenhouse gas emissions around the globe, leading to detriment of the environment as well [foo, b]. That being said, the supporting technologies of a Web 3.0 enabled smart city could be the enabler of reducing food waste and to build a more sustainable planet.

Over the decades the food production system - the way to get food from farm to the table in the household - has evolved to a complex network. Today's food production system provides the consumers more variety, convenient, economical and healthier source of food, however, such a system comes with its own challenges, such as the case where ingredients produced by one producer could end up in thousands of other products distributed in many different shops [Yiannas, 2018, Zhao et al., 2019]. This challenge is an issue of food safety, which is potentially detrimental to consumers' health and seriously damage the consumer's trust on the food market. For example, some immoral food producer could use trench oil to produce cooking oil, which is then distributed to thousands of shops, which is retrospectively bought and consumed by the consumer, making them sick in the process. Several cases of such accidents or food safety scandals such as "horsemeat scandal" "Sudan red", "clenbuterol", "Sanlu toxic milk powder" and "trench oil" [Tian, 2016] have happened all over the world. These scandals not just harm the economy of the food market, but at the same time threaten the safety and stability of the society as well. Although there are standards available such as General Food Law in EU [foo, d], Food Safety Modernization Act (FSMA) in US [fms,], which try to standardize traceability of digital information of food production in some of the stages of food supply chain, these standards are regional and currently there is no holistic standardization of tracking and recording data for food traceability purposes in all stages of food supply chain across the globe. Henceforth, in order to deal with such a challenge related to food safety, Blockchain Technology (BT) [Dey, 2018a, Dey, 2018b] may play a vital role in the traceability of food ingredients in recent times such that the consumers can trace the source of the food ingredients that they are buying/consuming.

Traditionally, many producers still record data of their production on papers, whereas, some producers digitize the production data, which doesn't enable interaction with other parties in the food system. Moreover, traditional food production systems are centralized in nature and could result in the trust problem, such as fraud, corruption, tampering and falsifying information. During a food-borne outbreak, sifting through thousands of documents (digital or paper) to trace food ingredients could be slow and complicated. In recent times, several methodologies [Tian, 2016, Zhao et al., 2019, Astill et al., 2019, Kamble et al., 2020] based on BT have been proposed to solve the challenge of food traceability for food safety purposes. The key strengths of utilizing BT is its decentralized, distributed and trusted nature, which could be advantageously used for food traceability and transparency for consumers at any point of the food production system. However, all the proposed BT frameworks [Tian, 2016, Zhao et al., 2019, Astill et al., 2019, Kamble et al., 2020] only deal with effective traceability of food supply chains, but not with technical solutions to make the food traceability more accessible to consumers such that they can verify and track their bought food items, may be with an easy-to-access device such as a mobile phone [Dey et al., 2019a, Dey et al., 2020a, Dey et al., 2019b, Dey et al., 2020b].

| (a) UPC Barcode | (b) Details corresponding UPC |

Figure 2.2: UPC barcode for Tropicana Trop50 Blackberry Cherry juice as fetched from BarcodeSpider.com [bar, b]

On the other hand, a popular way to store food data digitally is by using 1D barcodes such as Universal Product Code barcode [bar, a, Drobnik, 2015]. The Universal Product Code (UPC) barcode consists of 12 numeric digits that are uniquely assigned to each trade/food item. Every region or country maintains a database which holds the record of these trade/food items along with the UPC unique code, which are capable of storing the following data: the type of product, size, manufacturer and the country of origin of the food item. Therefore, if a consumer wants to know more about the bought food item, they have to use a barcode reader (using mobile phone application), which will fetch the unique UPC from the barcode and then fetch the information from an online database using the UPC. Although the information is fetched from an online database, the amount of information available on the item is limited to the type of product, size, manufacturer and the country of origin based on the type of the database. Therefore, no accurate traceability of the item throughout the supply chain is available for the consumer to verify. For example, Fig. 2.2.(a) represents a typical 1D barcode, which accompanies the Tropicana juice's product label [bar, b], and only reflects the following information (see Fig. 2.2.(b)) about the product: UPC number, European Article Number (EAN), Amazon Standard Identification Number (ASIN) product category, brand, model and last scan date-time, as fetched from BarcodeSpider.com. It should be kept in mind that the 1D barcode in Fig. 2.2.(a) only allows to store 12 digit UPC and no other information, therefore, if the correct database is not used to fetch the information on the product using UPC then the information might not get retrieved at all. Moreover, if the consumer is not connected to the Internet, s/he might not even retrieve any information based on the UPC by scanning traditional 1D barcode since a lookup on the online database using UPC is necessary.

Another issue is that many food products have shorter shelf life such as fresh vegetables and fruits should be consumed within few weeks of being produced and the expiry/best before date is printed on the label of the food item during the packaging and hence, is not available in the UPC barcode information. Many food management applications [nos, ,now,] are now being offered to remind the consumer of the expiry/best before dates of the food products to reduce food waste in the household. In these applications (apps), a consumer can record the bought food items along with their expiry/best before dates, to create a reminder to consume the items before they expire. These applications offer barcode scanning to automatically enter the bought food items in to the apps, however, given the lack of information stored in the barcode, the consumer still has to enter the expiry/best before date of each items individually. Therefore, this calls for a technology which enables the consumer not just to be able to verify the source of the bought food items throughout the supply chain for food traceability purposes, but also automatically fetch the respective expiry/best before date.

Several studies [Tian, 2016, Zhao et al., 2019, Astill et al., 2019, Kamble et al., 2020] have been proposed over the years to utilize blockchain and other technologies such as QR code in conjunction to digitize food supply chain data for traceability purposes. Moreover, studies [Yiannas, 2018, Marin et al., 2021] using blockchain to raise awareness of food waste are also being proposed. However, none of the published studies use blockchain, QR code, cloud computing and machine learning in conjunction to develop a framework that could reduce food waste.

To reduce food waste and improve traceability for food safety, we face two distinct challenges:

1. Digitizing food supply chain data such that the food data can be accessed easily for improved traceability.

2. Using machine learning to learn patterns from the digitized food supply chain data and optimize waste.

We overcome the first challenge we propose *FoodSQRBlock* (Food **S**afety **Q**uick **R**esponse **Block**) [Dey et al., 2021], a BT based framework, which digitizes the food production information such that the consumer and producers can trace the food produce at any point of the food production system, and make the information easily accessible using Quick Response code (QR code) such that the information can be retrieved and verified easily by the consumers and producers. In this book, we also provide a proposal for a large scale integration of FoodSQRBlock in the cloud such that the framework could be adopted easily given the improvement and accessibility of cloud technology.

To overcome the second challenge we propose *SmartNoshWaste* [Dey et al., 2022] - a Blockchain based multi-layered framework utilizing machine learning (more specifically reinforcement learning), cloud computing and QR code in a decentralized Web 3.0 enabled smart city. Blockchain is an excellent technology to digitize and decentralize food supply chain data, whereas, QR code could be utilized in concurrence to make the digitized data more accessible to consumers, especially via smartphones. We have chosen cloud computing for the framework to improve the speed of computation to provide a seamless user experience in validating and accessing the data. Also, cloud computing improves maintainability of software development as the changes in the software could be easily pushed on to the server for it to effect. On the other hand, machine learning being a sub field of AI, where the computing machine improves automatically through experience and by the use of data [Mitchell, 1997], such a mechanism can be utilized to learn from the data and henceforth, optimize food waste.

SmartNoshWaste has two layers: 1) *Data System Architecture* and 2) *Machine Learning Module*. The goal of the *Data System Architecture* is to digitize and store food data on the Blockchain using QR code and cloud computing to improve traceability and accessibility of such data and such that intelligence could be used by agents (machines) to reduce waste in *Machine Learning Module*. To the best of our knowledge this is the first framework to be proposed using Blockchain, cloud computing, QR code and machine learning in conjunction in a Web 3.0 enabled smart city to reduce food waste.

In the following chapter, we are going to explore some of the key concepts such as Blockchain, AI, QR Code and Cloud Computing that are prerequisite to understanding FoodSQRBlock and SmartNoshWaste frameworks.

Chapter 3

Prerequisite: Blockchain, AI, QR Code and Cloud Computing

In this chapter, we explore some of the key concepts and technologies used to develop the FoodSQRBlock and SmartNoshWaste frameworks.

3.0.1 Blockchain Technology

When Satoshi Nakamoto [Dey, 2018b] released the technology named Bitcoin, he revolutionised the industry not because he had invented a new currency system, which does not require intervention of institutional mediator while transferring money from one entity to another, but because he had gifted one of the most disruptive technologies, which has come to life in decades. With the introduction of Bitcoin, Blockchain got introduced to the world, which is a digital ledger in which all transactions are recorded chronologically and publicly. But the application of blockchain is not just limited to crypto-currencies [blo, a, blo, b] such as Bitcoin and have proved to be useful in tracking ownership, provenance of documents, digital assets, physical assets, voting rights, etc. Blockchain network is traditionally of three types as follows:

1. **Public**: In this network, everyone can check and verify the transaction made. The network is also open to anyone who wants to participate in the consensus process.

2. **Private**: In this type of network, strict restrictions are applied on data access and the nodes (user/entity) have restricted access to specific block chains, which are monitored by a governing body.

3. **Consortium**: Nodes in this type of network can form partnership with businesses or other authorities. This type of network may be public or private and hence, this could be seen as a hybrid approach as partly decentralized.

Blockchain Technology is popular because of its design features, which are composed of six key elements as follows:

1. **Decentralized**: Blockchain data could be recorded, stored, updated and distributed without depending on a central authority or node.

2. **Transparency**: Data recorded and stored are transparent and are visible. Therefore, leveraging trust among its users.

3. **Open Source**: The source code as well as the most of the blockchain dependent systems are open to view, free to use and provide the ease of extension for other applications.

4. **Autonomous**: Blockchain updates are consensus based and thus data could be updated securely from a single user to the whole system. This feature provides autonomy to the system to update data securely.

5. **Immutability**: All data in the blockchain are reserved forever.

6. **Anonymity**: Blockchain also provides anonymity to its users and make the system more trust worthy by only using the users' blockchain addresses instead of their personal information.

3.0.2 AI and Reinforcement Learning

Artificial Intelligence or AI [Winston, 1992] is the field of study to enable computing machines to perform tasks that are commonly associated with intelligent beings like humans. On the other hand, Machine Learning or ML [El Naqa and Murphy, 2015] is a sub-field of AI where the computing machine can improve automatically through experience and by the use of data. Traditionally, ML could be broadly categorized into: Supervised [Singh et al., 2016], Unsupervised [Gentleman and Carey, 2008] and Reinforcement learning [Sutton and Barto, 2018]. Out of these, reinforcement learning has become a popular choice among researchers as we move towards Artificial General Intelligence (AGI) [Goertzel and Pennachin, 2007]. Artificial general intelligence is the hypothetical ability of an intelligent agent (computing machine) that is capable of understanding or learning any intellectual task that a human being can.

Moreover, reinforcement learning (RL) is a type of machine learning algorithm, where an intelligent agent, which is a computing system that perceives its environment to take actions autonomously in order to achieve cumulative rewards based on the knowledge gathered from the environment. Fig. 3.1 shows a representative diagram of an intelligent agent. Here, reward could be optimizing performance or power consumption or thermal efficiency or combination of these together.

3.0.3 QR Code

QR code [Dey et al., 2012b, Huang et al., 2020, Dey, 2012, Dey et al., 2012b, Dey et al., 2013] is an effective information transmission medium, which is widely used in product traceability, advertising, mobile payment, passport verification and other fields. QR code is defined into 40 symbol versions (to carry various data payloads) and 4 user-selectable error correction level (ECL): L, M, Q and H, which can correct up to 7%, 15%, 25% and 30% error codewords respectively when attacked by defacement. The larger QR version can offer higher data payload where the QR code can hold a maximum capacity of 2,956 bytes for a version 40 code. The error correction capability of QR code is one of the key features of this type of barcode introduced by QR code standard and allows the barcode reader to retrieve the data correctly if portions of the barcode are damaged. QR code utilizes Reed-Solomon error correction algorithm to realize this fault tolerance, where the error correction codewords would be generated by Reed-Solomon algorithm and added

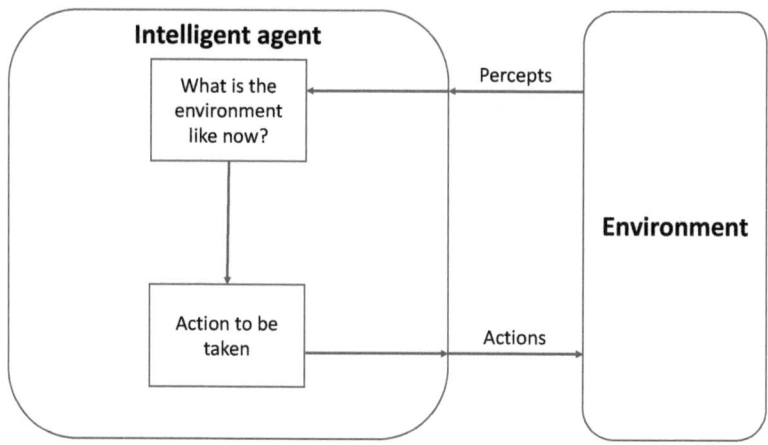

Figure 3.1: Representative diagram of intelligent agent

in the tail of QR code data codewords [Dey et al., 2013, Dey et al., 2012a, Lin, 2016, Dey, 2013]. Usually two error correction codewords could be used to correct codeword data error. Obviously, the larger the QR code version and the error correction level, it can offer higher data payload and reliability. Fig. 3.2 represents a QR code in which a simple, "Hello, World!" message is embedded.

Figure 3.2: Representational QR code with "Hello, World!" message embedding

3.0.4 Cloud Computing

Cloud computing (cloud) [De Donno et al., 2019, Qi and Tao, 2019] is a model to enable ubiquitous, convenient, on-demand network access to a shared pool of configurable computing resources such as networks, servers, storage, applications, and services, which can be rapidly provisioned and released with minimal management effort or service provider interaction [Bohn et al., 2011]. The essential characteristics of Cloud computing are summarized as follows:

1. **On-demand self-service**: For cloud computing, capabilities can be provided automatically when needed, without requiring any human interaction between the consumer and the service provider.

2. **Broad network access**: In this type of service, computing capabilities are available over the network and accessible through several mechanisms disposable for a wide range of consumer platforms such as workstations, laptops, and smartphones.

3. **Resource pooling**: In cloud, computing resources are pooled to accommodate multiple consumers, and hence, dynamically allocating and deallocating them according to consumer's demand. Moreover, the provider resources are location independent, i.e. the consumer does not have any knowledge or control of their exact location.

4. **Rapid elasticity**: In cloud, computing capabilities can be provided flexibly and released to scale in and out according to the consumer's demand. Therefore, the consumer has the perception of unlimited, and always adequate, computing capabilities.

5. **Measured service**: In cloud, resource usage can be monitored and reported according to the type of service being offered. This is particularly relevant in pay-per-use, or pay-per-user services because it grants a great transparency between the provider and the consumer of such services.

Cloud services can be provided to consumers in a variety of ways, and one such service is Software as a service (SaaS) [Ali et al., 2019], where the software and its related data are centrally hosted in the cloud computing environment such that the software could be provided to numerous consumers.

In the following chapter, we explore the FoodSQRBlock, which aims to digitize the food supply chain data such that the data could be easily traceable and accessible for improved food safety and to train the machine learning model to optimize waste in the supply chain.

Chapter 4

FoodSQRBlock: FoodSQRBlock: Digitizing Food Production and the Supply Chain Data

In this chapter, we introduce FoodSQRBlock (**Food Safety Quick Response Block**), a blockchain technology based framework, which digitizes the food production information, and makes it easily accessible, traceable and verifiable by the consumers and producers by using QR codes. We also show a large scale integration of FoodSQRBlock in the cloud to show the feasibility and scalability of the framework, and experimental evaluation to prove that.

4.1 Proposed Framework: FoodSQRBlock

In order to design BT based framework to make food supply chain or food production data more traceable and accessible, first, we have to analyze the different phases and activities present within a generic food supply chain. In our proposed framework, we focus our research on Farm-to-Fork supply chain, which has five main phases [Baralla et al., 2019] characterizing a generic food supply chain, as follows.

- **Production**: This is the primary production phase which represents all the activities related to agriculture within the farm.

- **Processing**: In this phase, harvesting the produce into products is performed. Preparation and packaging of the produce is also performed in this phase, where each package is uniquely identified trough a production batch code.

- **Distribution**: In this phase, once the product is packaged and labeled, it is released for distribution to different warehouses and other distribution centers for product storage.

- **Retailing**: In this phase, the products are delivered to the retailers, who sell the products to the consumers, from the distribution centers.

- **Consumption**: The consumer is the end user of the food supply chain, where s/he buys the product and requires the quality standards verifying traceability and access other relevant data about the product such as the expiry date.

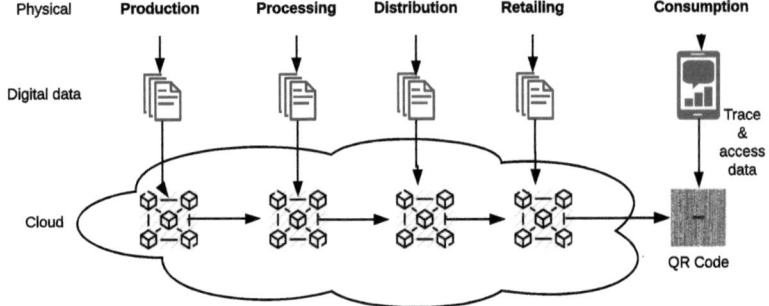

Figure 4.1: Overview of the System Architecture of FoodSQRBlock based on Farm-to-Fork supply chain

In our proposed framework, FoodSQRBlock, we focus on digitizing data from the first four phases (production, processing, distribution and retailing) and then use these data in the BT for traceability and accessibility by the consumer in the consumption phase. All digital data regarding the first four phases will be recorded and maintained in the blockchain in the cloud.

System Architecture: To design our BT framework we propose a multilevel system, whose architecture is represented in Fig. 5.1. Our system has three layers as follows.

- **Physical layer**: This layers consists of different food products from different farmers and producers within the supply chain.

- **Digital data layer**: This layer includes every single digital data associated with the produce belonging to the physical layer, which will be used for traceability and accessibility. One example of data about the produce could be the expiry date of the food product.

- **Cloud layer**: In this layer, the digital data is processed in the Cloud using BT, which is used for traceability and accessibility.

Now, we introduce our FoodSQRBlock framework with an example to digitize the food production data at the four different phases (production, processing, distribution & retailing) of the supply chain and make the data available and accessible to consumers (consumption) for verification purposes using QR code. Fig. 4.2 shows the exemplar conceptual FoodSQRBlock framework of an agri-food supply chain traceability system. For this exemplar supply chain we have considered the production and processing phases to happen in the farm, whereas, the warehouse represents the distribution phase and the shops represent the retailing phase. In Fig. 4.2, the food item is produced and processed in a farm, where the relevant information are digitized and stored in block (genesis block/block 0) and then the item is transported to a warehouse/distribution center, from where the item is finally transported to a shop for consumers to buy. In each step/phase of this supply chain, a new block is created which stores the hash of the previous block such that at any point the item (produce) could be tracked and traced. We utilize SHA256 algorithm [Irving and Holden, 2016], which is very popular in BT nowadays, for the hash function to generate the hash of the previous block. In our FoodSQR-Block, we utilize SHA256 for the hash function since it provides the required security for the associated computational cost on the cloud. If we utilize a different hashing algorithm such as SHA512, it is computationally more expensive and takes longer to compute on the cloud, which ultimately increases the computational cost, especially if thousands of digital data of the produce are processed on the cloud every day.

Within the FoodSQRBlock we have two modules: *Encoding* & *Decoding*. The Encoding module digitizes the produce information, generates the blocks and also generates the QR code holding the information. The Decode module, which is an open source software (algorithm), enables the consumers to fetch and verify the information about the produce. The program source code for Encoding and Decoding modules are provided in Sec. **??**.

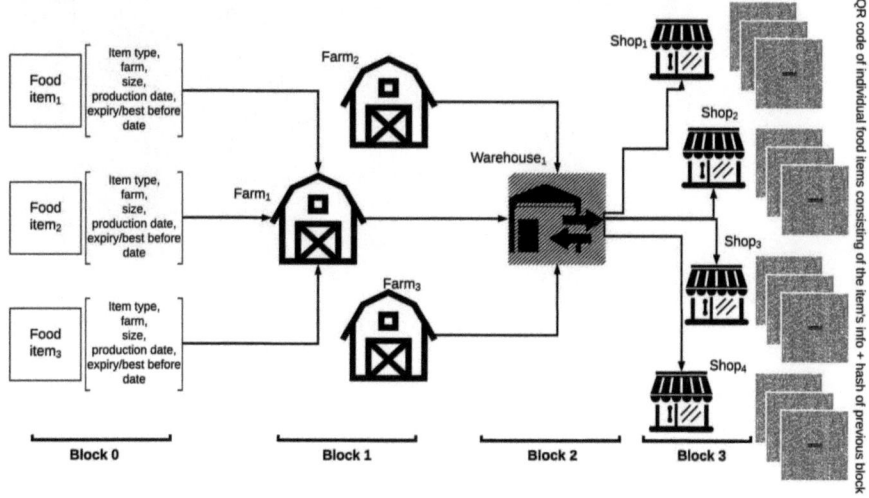

Figure 4.2: Conceptual FoodSQRBlock framework of an agri-food supply chain traceability system based on QR code & blockchain technology

Encoding Module: If we consider f_i as the i_{th} instance of the food item being produced at a farm or manufacturing plant, then the following information ($info(f_i)$) about the produce: produce name (p_i), type (t_i), farm/manufacturing plant id ($farm_i$), size of produce (s_i), production date ($pdate_i$), expiry/best before date ($edate_i$), could be digitized such that these information could be passed along with the block for traceability and verification purposes by the consumer. Therefore, the digitized information could be represented as follows:

$$info(f_i) = \{p_i, t_i, farm_i, s_i, pdate_i, edate_i\} \tag{4.1}$$

In $info(f_i)$, the unique farm id ($farm_i$) is stored, which correlates with the farm data (farm name, Geo-location of the farm), stored in a database maintaining records of all the farms/manufacturing plants. Here, the unique farm id is also generated using

13

the hash function on the stored details of the farm/manufacturing plant, and hence, ensuring that the farm id is unique for each farm. In the genesis block (block 0), $info(f_i)$ is stored. Whenever the produce is transported or processed by an entity in the supply chain a new block is generated, which holds the original $info(f_i)$ as well as the hash of the previous block. QR code could be generated at any point in the supply chain and it holds the information passed in the block ($info(f_i)$ and hash of previous block). Fig. 4.3.(a) shows the QR code generated at the shop when the produced milk is transported to the shop (from farm to warehouse/distribution center to shop).

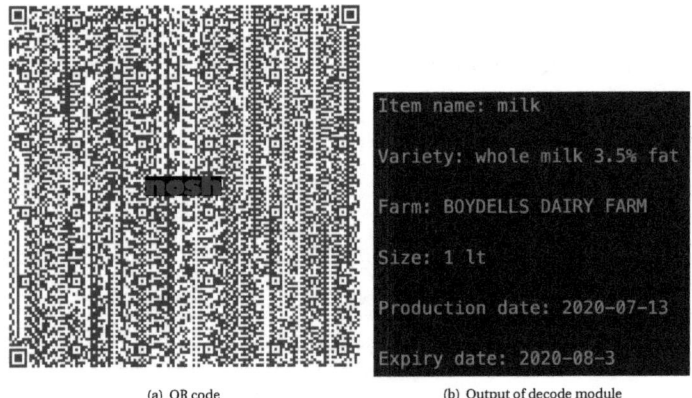

(a) QR code   (b) Output of decode module

Figure 4.3: QR code holding information of a dairy product, which is produced at Boydells Dairy Farm in the UK, generated by FoodSQRBlock

Decoding Module: In this module, the information ($info(f_i)$) and the hash of the previous block are fetched using a QR code scanner (smartphone) from the QR code. Since, the information of the previous block is made available online for the consumers to verify, the Decode module performs a hash function on the information from the previous block and compares the value with the hash value fetched from the QR code. If the hash values match then it means the information about the produce is authentic (leveraging immutability characteristic of BT). A reverse search on the unique farm id fetched from the QR code is performed to fetch the details of the farm/manufacturing plant where the produce originated and the information is displayed to the consumer along with other information about the produce ($p_i, t_i, s_i, pdate_i, edate_i$). Since, the details of the farm/manufacturing plant is stored in a database, the reverse search on the database could be performed using the unique farm id. Fig. 4.3.(b) shows the decoded information about the dairy product, fetched from the QR code in Fig. 4.3.(a).

Note: Given the storage capacity of QR codes, more information could be stored/embedded in the QR code in the Encoding module. As a proof of concept and to test run Food-SQRBlock framework, we found $info(f_i)$ embedding $p_i, t_i, farm_i, s_i, pdate_i, edate_i$ are most suitable for the purpose.

4.2 Experimental evaluation: case study & large scale integration of FoodSQRBlock

In order to implement and evaluate the FoodSQRBlock in the cloud, we chose Google Cloud Platform (GCP)'s [Krishnan and Gonzalez, 2015] Compute Engine service, which is a virtual machine consisting of 8 vCPUs, 16 GB RAM memory and 500 GB disk memory space, to setup our cloud server. The Compute Engine was running on Debian GNU OS (Linux) version 10 (code name "buster"). We chose the following two food items to test run our implementation: *milk* & *pumpkin*. Milk is sourced from a local farm (Boydells Dairy Farm in Essex, UK) and pumpkin is also sourced locally (Foxes Farm Produce in Essex, UK). The milk is sourced from the farm and then sold directly in the farmer's market, whereas, the pumpkins are moved to a warehouse distributing facility after being sourced from the farm and then were sold in the farmer's market. We implemented the FoodSQRBlock as a webservice (SaaS) on the GCP Compute Engine server to process the blocks and generate QR code, containing all the relevant information, for individual produce. We simulated the production in the aforementioned farms (Boydells Dairy Farm & Foxes Farm Produce) in the cloud platform to replicate the scenario of a real world food production system. For a batch of milk being sourced around the same time, are all accumulated into the same block and blockchain consisting of two blocks (genesis block and hash of genesis block) are generated for each individual batch. Whereas, for pumpkins, every one hundred pumpkins are accumulated into the same block and since, each batch of pumpkin made it to farmer's market (shop) via distribution center, each batch was processed to consist of 3 blocks in the chain (genesis block, hash of genesis block when it went to distribution center and hash of the block from distribution center after making it to the farmer's market).

4.2.1 Experimental Evaluation

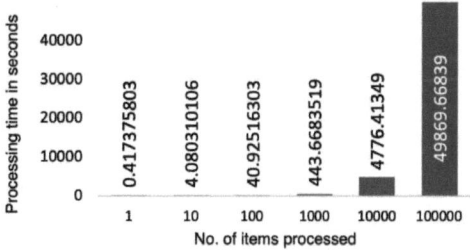

Figure 4.4: Time taken to process different number of items (using FoodSQRBlock) in Google Cloud Platform's Compute Engine

In the GCP's Compute Engine, the webservice of FoodSQRBlock processed (generate hash of block along with stored information as mentioned in the Encoding module in Sec. 5.1) different numbers of produce to see the time taken for processing such information. Fig. 4.4 shows the processing time in seconds for 1, 10, 100, 1000, 10000, 100000 number of produces on the GCP's Compute Engine.

4.2.2 Analysis & Discussion

From Sec. 4.2.1 it is evident that given the resources of GCP's Compute Engine, 10,000 items could be processed easily under 80 minutes. However, if a farm or manufacturing plant produces more than 10,000 items in a day then a more computationally powerful cloud server is required to be able to process the items within a reasonable time. Because GCP allows flexible ad-hoc computation resources for its Compute Engine, it is easy for us to scale up or down based on the numbers of items to be processed, therefore, solving the storage capacity issue of BT.

It should also be kept in mind that currently there is no standards or regulations on standardize traceability of digital information of food production across the globe and henceforth, implementation of the proposed FoodSQRBlock would require collaboration across regions.

4.3 Future Direction and Discussion

AI optimization: Food production process could be complicated depending on the region or country. Every year 1.3 billion tons of food are wasted and a lot of the food waste come from the production level. Artificial Intelligence (AI) could be utilized to optimize the production/quantity of food produced at the farm using the end consumer data that is connected to the FoodSQRBlock.

Bottleneck over Cloud: One of the limitations of utilizing BT in the cloud for food security is the lack of agreement between food producers and governments across regions/countries. Henceforth, implementation of the proposed FoodSQRBlock could vary from region to region and country to country based on the local regulations and legislations revolving food security. Such a difference in implementation in the architecture could introduce bottlenecks in the performance over the cloud and it would be interesting to research in those areas such as diffusion of BT over different regions/countries to come up with solutions to overcome the challenges faced accordingly.

Security: Given the fact that slightly different implementation of FoodSQRBlock could lead to different security flaws that have not been explored yet, it would be another possible area to focus our future research direction.

4.4 Summary

In this chapter, we introduce FoodSQRBlock, a blockchain technology based framework, which digitizes the food production information, and makes it easily accessible, traceable and verifiable by the consumers and producers by using QR codes to embed the information. We also implemented FoodSQRBlock in Google Cloud Platform to replicate a real life food production scenario using milk & pumpkins as produce examples from real farms in the UK. Experimental evaluation proves the feasibility and scalability of FoodSQRBlock implementation in the cloud. In the next chapter, we introduce SmartNoshWaste framework to implement machine learning on top of FoodSQRBlock framework to reduce waste in the food supply chain.

Chapter 5

SmartNoshWaste: Using Blockchain & Machine Learning in Food Supply Chain to Reduce Waste

In this chapter, we explore SmartNoshWaste - a blockchain based multi-layered framework utilizing cloud computing, QR code and reinforcement learning to reduce food waste. We also evaluate SmartNoshWaste on real world food data collected from the nosh app to show the efficacy of the proposed framework and we are able to reduce food waste by 9.46% in comparison to the originally collected food data based on the experimental evaluation.

5.1 Proposed Framework: SmartNoshWaste

SmartNoshWaste is an extension of our FoodSQRBlock framework. FoodSQRBlock framework digitizes the food supply chain data such that data at the consumer end in a Farm-to-Fork supply chain model is easily accessible by the consumer for traceability. However, the FoodSQRBlock framework lacked one key component as follows: it did not focus on reducing food wastage based on the data from the supply chain. SmartNosh-Waste is built as an extension of FoodSQRBlock to resolve this.

Our SmartNoshWaste framework has two distinct layers: 1) Data System Architecture and 2) Machine Learning Module. In the Data System Architecture we utilize BT, QR code and cloud computing to digitize and store the food data such that it can be used in the Machine Learning Module to minimize food wastage.

5.1.1 Assumptions and data system architecture of SmartNoshWaste

In order to design blockchain based framework to minimize food waste, first, we have to digitize food production data such that it is more traceable and accessible at all stages of the supply chain. To achieve this we have to analyze the different phases and activities present within a generic food supply chain. In our proposed framework, we focus our research on Farm-to-Fork supply chain, which has five main phases/stages [Baralla et al., 2019] identifying a generic food supply chain, consisting of *Production, Processing, Distribution, Retailing and Consumption*.

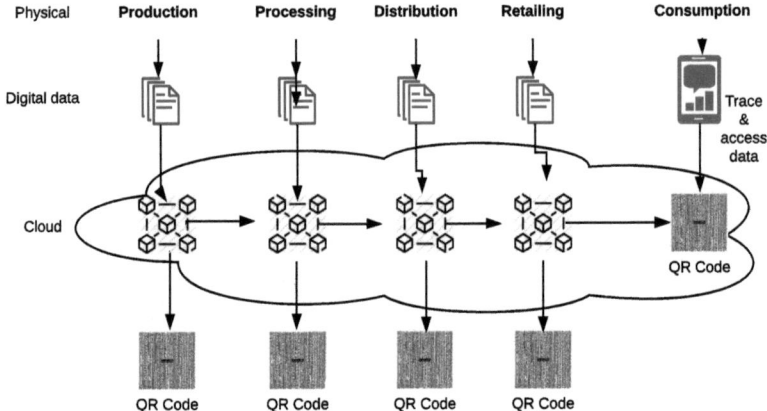

Figure 5.1: Overview of the Data System Architecture of SmartNoshWaste based on Farm-to-Fork supply chain

In our proposed framework, SmartNoshWaste, first, we aim to digitizing data from the five aforementioned phases (production, processing, distribution, retailing and consumption). After the digitization of the supply chain data we store the data on the BT for traceability and accessibility by the stakeholders in any phase including farmers and consumers. All digital data regarding the five phases will be recorded and maintained on the blockchain in the cloud. Cloud computing service is chosen for two specific purposes: 1) to improve the computational speed of the processing and transactions on the blockchain; 2) any changes made to the software side of the SmartNoshWaste framework could be easily deployed by the developers across different regions.

Data System Architecture: To design our BT framework we propose a multilevel system, whose architecture is represented in Fig. 5.1. Our system has three layers as follows.

- **Physical layer**: This layer comprises of different products from the supply chain from different farmers and producers.

- **Digital data layer**: This layer consists of every single digital data correlated to the produce belonging to the physical layer, which will be used for traceability and accessibility. Example of data about the produce could be the expiry date of the food product, the farm's identity where it was produced along with the production batch number.

- **Cloud layer**: In this layer, the digital data is processed in the Cloud using BT and made available using QR code at different phases, which is used for traceability and accessibility.

Data stored: Fig. 5.2 shows the generic data regarding the food item in different phases of the supply chain that are digitized in the digital data layer such that they can be

18

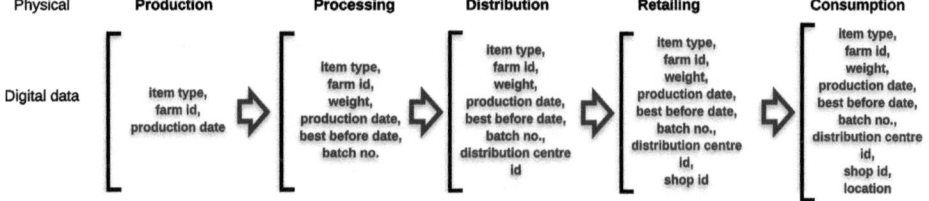

Figure 5.2: Generic data regarding food in different phases of the supply chain that are digitized to be stored in the blockchain

used/stored in the BT framework in the cloud layer. When the food item is produced in the farm the basic data that are stored are: item type, farm id and production date. However, as we progress in to different phases of the supply chain more information about the food item is added and stored in the blockchain. The relevant information about the food item from the production phase are digitized and stored in the genesis block/block 0 and then the item is transported to different phases of the supply chain. As the food item is transported and processed in different phases of the supply chain, more relevant data about the item is added and a new block is created in each phase to store them along with the hash of the previous block. The consumption phases in our proposed framework consist of the following data: item type, farm id, weight, production date, best before date, batch no., distribution centre id, shop id and location. These data can be modified and vary based on the unique requirements of the farm or processing centre or distributor or the country of produce. It should be noted that in order to safeguard the privacy of user, in the consumption phase we only store the geographical location data of the user/consumer tied with the food item data such that the user's true identity can't be revealed, however, consumption and wastage details about a particular food item can still be traced.

In each phase of this food supply chain, a new block of data is created, which stores the hash of the previous block such that at any point the food item/ingredient could be tracked and traced. In each step, the block data is also made available in the form of digital QR code (as shown in Fig. 5.1) such that the digital data about the item on the block is accessible easily to consumers or any stakeholders from any phase in the supply chain. We use the SHA256 algorithm [Irving and Holden, 2016], which is a very popular in blockchain nowadays for using the hash function to create the hash of the previous block. In our SmartNoshWaste, we use SHA256 for the hash function because it provides the desirable required security for the associated computational cost on the cloud. In case if we use a different hash function as in SHA512, then it is computationally more expensive and henceforth, takes longer to compute on the cloud. In case of using SHA512, it would ultimately increase the computational cost, especially given the fact that thousands of digital data of the food produce will be processed on the cloud every day based on the proposed framework.

Metric to quantify production: We also need to quantify the food production and wastage data such that they could be used by our machine learning module. We have assumed that the amount of food produced is based on consumption, surplus for food security and the amount wasted. In order to achieve this we propose a metric considering the production, consumption, surplus and wastage of a particular food item each week of each month in a quarter as follows.

$$P^i_{YYQXNM} = C^i_{YYQXNM} + S^i_{YYQXNM} + W^i_{YYQXNM} \qquad (5.1)$$

In Eq. 5.1, P, C, S and W are the total amount of produce for a particular food item, total amount of the food item consumed, the surplus of the food item kept for food security and the amount wasted of the food item respectively. In the equation, $YYQXN$ represents the year (YY) and the quarter (QXN, where $X \epsilon \{1, 2, 3, 4\}$, $N \epsilon \{1, 2, 3\}$ and $M \epsilon \{1, 2, 3, 4\}$) of the particular food item being produced respectively. This is to signify that there are four quarters (X) (Q1, Q2, Q3 and Q4) and each quarter consist of three months (N) and each month consists of 4 weeks approximately. A quarter is a three-month period on a company's financial calendar and we utilize the same concept in food production to quantify and track the data. In the equation, i signifies the respective phase in the food production supply chain (production, processing, distribution, retailing and consumption).

For each phases the Eq. 5.1 will look something as follows, starting from level 1 - production phase:

Production:

$$P^1_{YYQXN} = C^1_{YYQXNM} + S^1_{YYQXNM} + W^1_{YYQXNM} \qquad (5.2)$$

Processing:

$$P^2_{YYQXN} = C^2_{YYQXNM} + S^2_{YYQXNM} + W^2_{YYQXNM} \qquad (5.3)$$

Distribution:

$$P^3_{YYQXN} = C^3_{YYQXNM} + S^3_{YYQXNM} + W^3_{YYQXNM} \qquad (5.4)$$

Retailing:

$$P^4_{YYQXN} = C^4_{YYQXNM} + S^4_{YYQXNM} + W^4_{YYQXNM} \qquad (5.5)$$

Consumption:

$$P^5_{YYQXN} = C^5_{YYQXNM} + S^5_{YYQXNM} + W^5_{YYQXNM} \qquad (5.6)$$

It is also worth noting that except in the production phase the amount produced in processing, distribution, retailing and consumption maintains a direct relationship with the amount consumed, surplus produced and amount wasted of the food item in the previous phase. This could be denoted by the following equation.

$$C^{i-1}_{YYQXN} + S^{i-1}_{YYQXNM} + W^{i-1}_{YYQXNM} = P^i_{YYQXNM} \qquad (5.7)$$

Note: Though we are quantifying production, consumption, surplus and wastage of food, it should be kept in mind that in real world the food supply chain data can often vary due to unforeseen or unknown variables that could often include geographical and political issues. However, to propose a framework to minimize food waste using machine learning we have to make certain assumptions and henceforth, quantifying the data in the aforementioned approach. It should also be kept in mind that often times food wastage and loss is closely related to food surplus [Papargyropoulou et al., 2014, Teigiserova et al., 2020] in different phases of the supply chain. For this purpose, we try to minimize food surplus in a particular phase to minimize wastage.

5.1.2 Machine learning module of SmartNoshWaste

As part of the SmartNoshWaste framework we utilize Q-learning based reinforcement learning (RL) [Watkins and Dayan, 1992]. In Q-learning, the RL agent maintains a table consisting of actions (a) and states (s), where it can identify an optimal action-selection policy based on the Q function that the agent computes. The RL agent determines the environment (ϵ), in which the agent observes the state (s_t) at a given time instance t. Then it performs an action (a_t), and receives a reward (r_t) for that instance in ϵ. At every time instance (t^{th}), the agent chooses an action a_t from a predefined list of actions where $a_t \in 1, 2, ...K$ and K is the maximum number of actions allowed for a given state. Following the action at time t any changes are perceived in the ϵ are observed at time $t+1$, when the state of ϵ changes to s_{t+1}.

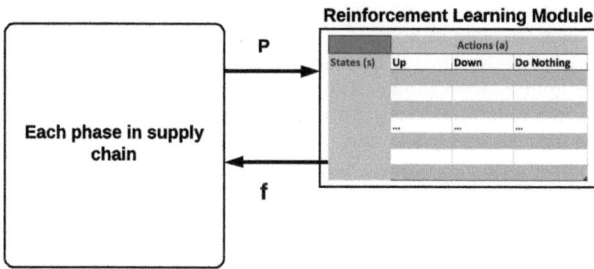

Figure 5.3: Diagramatic representation of Q-Learning based RL method in the Machine Learning Module of SmartNoshWaste

In SmartNoshWaste, the environment ϵ is the production amount (P^i_{YYQXNM}) of a food item in a particular phase consisting of a tuple of food consumption, surplus and wastage ($< C^{i-1}_{YYQXNM}, S^{i-1}_{YYQXNM}, W^{i-1}_{YYQXNM} >$) as per Eq. 5.1.

The goal of the RL agent is to maximize the reward r_t in the future. The propagation of information from the future is discounted by a factor called γ at every time step such that: $r_t = \sum_t^{t+n} \gamma_t r_t$ in order to lessen the reward's effect on the RL agent's choice of action. For every time step the probability that the agent chooses an action at a given state is defined by a policy function. In this policy, the function, which maximizes the agent's long term reward generation is called action-value function, which is defined by $Q(s_t, a_t)$ and is shown in Eq. 5.8.

$$Q(s_t, a_t) = Q(s_t, a_t) + \alpha(r_t - Q(s_t, a_t) + \gamma max_a Q(s_{t+1}, a)) \qquad (5.8)$$

In Eq. 5.8, α is the learning rate at which the agent learns new information. We have to keep in mind that the optimal $action - value$ function could be obtained by iteratively updating $Q(s_t, a_t)$ in Eq. 5.8. Now, in order to maximize the reward generation we would require a *reward function* ($R(s_t, a_t)$).

Since, food surplus leads to a lot of wastage if not consumed properly we try to minimize food surplus in order to minimize wastage. Given the fact that food production data is correlated to consumption, surplus and wastage (as shown in Eq. 5.1), if we consider a variable - f - that denotes the amount of food that should be reduced or increased in the food surplus to minimize wastage in that said phase of supply chain, we can modify Eq. 5.1 as follows.

$$P^i_{YYQXNM} = C^i_{YYQXNM} + (S^i_{YYQXNM} + f) + W^i_{YYQXNM} \qquad (5.9)$$

In Eq. 5.9, the value of f can be positive (UP), negative (Down) or zero (Do Nothing). Based on this equation, we can develop our reward function as follows.

$$R : minimize(W^i_{YYQXNM}) \longrightarrow S^i_{YYQXNM} + f \qquad (5.10)$$

The RL agent has three actions: Up (add the value of f to S^i_{YYQXNM}), Down (subtract the value of f to S^i_{YYQXNM}) and Do Nothing (value of f is set to zero). The actions in the RL agent are invoked depending on the initiator of the particular point in the phase. For our proposed technique, the actions are invoked every week.

Note: When we mention the goal to minimize food surplus, we keep in mind that the surplus is minimized not to threaten food security in that particular phase, however, only to minimize food wastage at that phase. RL agent is implemented locally, meaning that local optimization is performed in each phases of the supply chain to minimize food wastage. As per Eq. 5.1 and 5.7, since, production amount is correlated to the consumption, surplus and wastage amount of other phases in the supply chain, local optimization of wastage using RL agent would also lead to global optimization of wastage throughout all phases as well. The value of f in local optimization is defined or set by the initiator or manager of the particular point in the particular phase in the supply chain. For example, f value for a farm could be set by the farmer to minimize wastage in that farm, whereas, the f value in the retailing phase could be set by the shop owner to minimize wastage in the shop. These f values for different points in different phases could either be the same or different based on the requirements of consumption, surplus and wastage of that particular point in the phase. The f value after being used by the RL agent to find the minimized value of wastage in that particular phase, it could be used by the initiator or manager as a guiding amount to reduce waste. For example, if the f value by RL agent is computed as $x\%$ of the surplus, which should be reduced in the shop to achieve $y\%$ of wastage then the manager should reduce the surplus by $x\%$ in the next production cycle to achieve that reduction in waste goal.

5.2 Experimental evaluation: Case study with real food data

To evaluate the efficacy of our proposed SmartNoshWaste framework we implemented it on real data collected from the nosh app [nos,]. The nosh app is a food management app that helps the consumer to reduce food waste in their household by better managing their food consumption. The app comes will the capability to track the food items consumed or wasted in the week such that the user can make a more informed decision on what food to buy or not to buy the next time they go shopping. We focused on the data on "potato" collected worldwide via the nosh app. We chose to focus on data on potato because it is one of the most popular food items that is wasted, especially in the United Kingdom where the research team is located [foo, c]. The data collected are completely anonymized such that from the data user/consumer could not be identified, however, each food item data comes with geolocation tag such the consumption or wastage about

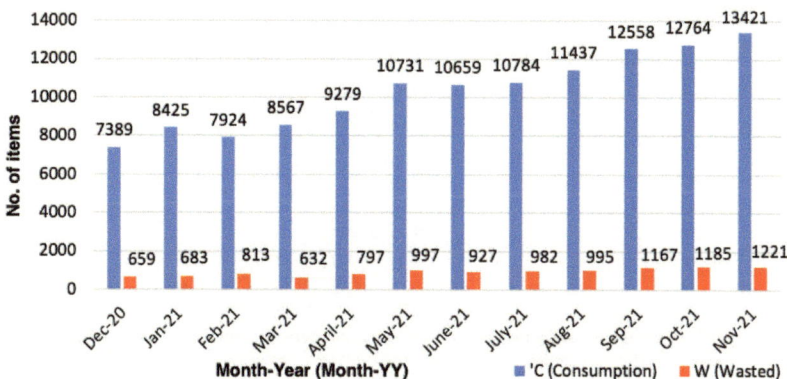

Figure 5.4: Consumption and wastage data on potatoes collected via the nosh app [nos,] where the Y-Axis represents the number of items consumed ($'C$) or wasted (W) and X-Axis represents the months of the year when the data was collected

the item could be tracked in a particular region. There were 134,996 potato consumption data collected worldwide via the nosh app over a 1 year period (December 2020 to November 2021). Fig. 5.4 shows the consumption and wastage data on potatoes collected via the nosh app, where the Y-Axis represents the number of items consumed ($'C$) or wasted (W) and X-Axis represents the months of the year when the data was collected. The nosh app was created to help consumer manage their food wastage occurring from overbuying and/or forgetting to consume the food before the "best before date" of the item. For this reason, the app collects data about consumption and wastage. The consumption data ($'C$) from the nosh app already considers the amount of food consumed by the user (C) and the surplus bought by the user (S), aiming to reduce waste by reducing the food surplus. Therefore, the consumption data from the nosh app can be denoted using the following equation.

$$'C^5_{YYQXNM} = C^5_{YYQXNM} + S^5_{YYQXNM} \tag{5.11}$$

In Eq. 5.11, $YYQXNM$ represents the year (YY) and the quarter (QXN, where $X\epsilon\{1,2,3,4\}$, $N\epsilon\{1,2,3\}$ and $M\epsilon\{1,2,3,4\}$) of the potato being consumed in the consumption phase (level 5) respectively. We evaluated SmartNoshWaste framework in the consumption phase, since, we use the data from the nosh app to find the desirable value of f that we need to subtract from the food surplus to achieve our minimal wastage goal. Our goal is to find f from the Machine Learning Module of SmartNoshWaste such that $'C^5_{YYQXNM} +$ ($-f$) leads to reduction in waste (W^5_{YYQXNM}) of potatoes for consumers. It should be noted that we aim to find the value of f that needs to be subtracted from $'C^5_{YYQXNM}$.

From Fig. 5.4 it should be noted that 123,938 amounts of potatoes were consumed whereas, 11,058 amounts of potatoes were wasted over the 12 month period. From the chart (Fig. 5.4) we can also notice that the average wastage over the months remained around 7% to 9% of the respective consumption for that month. Based on this knowledge we chose f value from 1 to 9 and evaluated our SmartNoshWaste's Machine Learning Module. We also predicted the percentage of potatoes that could be saved from being wasted compared to the amount of potatoes wasted over the 12 months period, which is collected from the nosh app. Table 5.1 shows the prediction data evaluated by the Ma-

	W'	O.W	R.W%
f=1	10900	11058	1.43
f=2	10786	11058	2.46
f=3	10693	11058	3.3
f=4	10542	11058	4.67
f=5	10482	11058	5.21
f=6	10351	11058	6.39
f=7	10232	11058	7.47
f=8	10099	11058	8.67
f=9	10012	11058	**9.46**

Table 5.1: Amount of potatoes saved over 12 months period for different f value, ranging from 1 to 9 and comparison between the original amount of potatoes wasted. W' represents the predicted amount of potatoes wasted based on the f value; $O.W$ represents the amount of potatoes wasted, which is collected from the nosh app; $R.W\%$ is the percentage of potatoes that could be saved, predicted by the Machine Learning Module of SmartNoshWaste.

chine Learning Module of SmartNoshWaste. In the table, W' represents the predicted amount of potatoes wasted based on the f value; $O.W$ represents the amount of potatoes wasted, which is collected from the nosh app; $R.W\%$ is the percentage of potatoes that could be saved, predicted by the Machine Learning Module of SmartNoshWaste. $R.W\%$ is calculated based on $\{(O.W - W')/O.W * 100\}$. From the Table 5.1 it is evident that we could potentially save 9.46% potatoes more compared to the original amount of potatoes wasted.

5.3 Future Direction and Discussion

There are several standards available related to food safety and traceability such as the General Food Law in the EU [foo, d] and the Food Safety Modernization Act (FSMA) [fms,] in the United States, which focus on standardizing the traceability of the digital food production information in some of the stages of the food supply chain. However, these standards are regional, and currently, there is no holistic standardization approach of the tracking and recording digital data for food traceability and waste purposes in all stages of the food supply chain across the globe. The proposed SmartNoshWaste aims to provide a general framework that can be implemented by academics and industry practitioners to reduce food waste despite geo-political and standardization difference across different regions around the globe.

Given the fact that SmartNoshWaste utilizes blockchain, QR code, cloud computing and machine learning in conjunction to tackle food waste, each technology involved in the framework comes with its own implementation issues based on the implementation of the framework by targeted software developer(s) in a particular region. As SmartNoshWaste aims to provide a holistic approach to use blockchain, QR code, cloud computing and machine learning in conjunction to tackle food waste, specific implementation challenges related to each of these associated technologies are not discusses in details as they would not fall within the scope of this research and framework proposal.

One of the key challenges of using blockchain in a smart city could be to prioritize privacy and data security of the citizens [Hakak et al., 2020]. If we look closely to some of the implementations of the smart city projects using blockchain in the practice then we could notice that regardless of using blockchain as a technology, the implementation to protect privacy and improve data security of citizens vary based on the available infrastructure of the respective project. Examples of such smart city projects in practice include French City Brain [fre,], Smart Dubai [dub,] and Limestone Network (Singaporean Startup) [sin,]. Keeping this in mind, while implementing SmartNoshWaste as part of the smart city, the stakeholders including software developer(s) might have to modify the blockchain network to improve the privacy and data security of its citizen based on the respective infrastructure of the smart city.

In section 5.1.1, we have used digital QR code to make the food data from each phases of the supply chain accessible and traceable by every stakeholders including the consumer. Though QR code has really good resistance against defacement or error correction in case of wear and tear of the physical print of QR codes, it should be kept in mind that based on the implementation of the QR code security of protecting the data embedded in the QR code will also vary. For example, physical printouts of QR code could be vulnerable to man-in-the-middle attack, by replacing the legitimate QR code by a fake one. Or the payload in the QR code could also be replaced by misrepresented payload, henceforth, damaging the integrity of the data stored within the QR code to be accessible to the stakeholders [QRc,]. To avoid these challenges we have implemented our QR code in digital form, which could be verified over a mobile platform including smartphones, tablets, etc. Moreover, to avoid earlier mentioned malpractice the exact implementation of the QR code would depend on the available infrastructure of the smart city and the implementation by the developers.

Another point to keep in mind that we have used Q-learning (Q-table) based reinforcement learning, which is a type of delayed reinforcement learning, where the reward is delayed till a better understanding of the enthronement is gathered through actions by the intelligent agent [Kaelbling et al., 1996]. Such type of machine learning algorithm depends on training the agent for a sufficient time to meet convergence. However, there are better machine learning algorithms that could improve this shortcoming and could lead to better rewards with less execution time and memory space. One such model could be Deep Q-Learning [Gu et al., 2016], where deep neural network is used with Q-table to map input states to the action and Q-value pair.

5.4 Summary

In this chapter, we explore SmartNoshWaste, which is a blockchain based multi-layered framework utilizing cloud computing, QR code and reinforcement learning in conjunction to reduce food waste in a decentralized Web 3.0 enabled smart city. As part of SmartNoshWaste we have also proposed a metric to quantify food production and waste data in the supply chain. Experimental evaluation of SmartNoshWaste on real data of potatoes collected from the nosh app shows the framework is capable of reducing food waste by 9.46% more compared to the potatoes wasted according to the nosh app.

Bibliography

[blo, a] Blockchain is useful for a lot more than bitcoin. http://theconversation.com/blockchain-is-useful-fora-lot-more-than-just-bitcoin-58921. Accessed: 2020-07-07.

[foo, a] Food loss and food waste. https://www.fao.org/food-loss-and-food-waste/flw-data. Accessed: 2021-12-22.

[fms,] Food safety modernization act (fsma). https://www.fda.gov/food/guidance-regulation-food-and-dietary-supplements/food-safety-modernization-act-fsma. Accessed: 2020-06-26.

[foo, b] Food waste: digesting the impact on climate. https://www.newfoodmagazine.com/article/153960/food-waste-climate/. Accessed: 2021-12-22.

[foo, c] Food waste facts and statistics. https://www.theecoexperts.co.uk/home-hub/food-waste-facts-and-statistics. Accessed: 2021-12-22.

[fre,] French city brain. https://frenchcitybrain.com/en/. Accessed: 2020-06-26.

[foo, d] General food law. https://ec.europa.eu/food/safety/general_food_law_en. Accessed: 2020-06-26.

[blo, b] How could blockchain be used in the enterprise. https://www.computerworlduk.com/galleries/security/how-could-blockchain-be-used-the-enterprise3628558/. Accessed: 2020-07-07.

[sin,] Limestone network (singaporean startup). https://limestone.network/. Accessed: 2020-06-26.

[nos,] nosh - food stock management. https://nosh.tech. Accessed: 2020-07-07.

[now,] Nowaste - food inventory list. https://www.nowasteapp.com. Accessed: 2020-07-07.

[QRc,] Qr codes and security. https://mobilephonesecurity.org/2011/09/qr-codes-and-security-my-take-html/. Accessed: 2020-06-26.

[dub,] Smart dubai. https://www.digitaldubai.ae/. Accessed: 2020-06-26.

[bar, a] Teach ict - barcodes. https://biturl.top/QJzuYz. Accessed: 2020-07-07.

[bar, b] Upc 704660784002 lookup. https://www.barcodespider.com/ 704660784002. Accessed: 2020-07-07.

[Alabdulwahhab, 2018] Alabdulwahhab, F. A. (2018). Web 3.0: the decentralized web blockchain networks and protocol innovation. In *2018 1st International Conference on Computer Applications & Information Security (ICCAIS)*, pages 1–4. IEEE.

[Ali et al., 2019] Ali, A. Q., Sultan, A. B. M., Abd Ghani, A. A., and Zulzalil, H. (2019). A systematic mapping study on the customization solutions of software as a service applications. *IEEE Access*, 7:88196–88217.

[Astill et al., 2019] Astill, J., Dara, R. A., Campbell, M., Farber, J. M., Fraser, E. D., Sharif, S., and Yada, R. Y. (2019). Transparency in food supply chains: A review of enabling technology solutions. *Trends in Food Science & Technology*, 91:240–247.

[Baralla et al., 2019] Baralla, G. et al. (2019). Ensure traceability in european food supply chain by using a blockchain system. In *2019 IEEE/ACM 2nd International Workshop on Emerging Trends in Software Engineering for Blockchain (WETSEB)*. IEEE.

[Batty et al., 2012] Batty, M., Axhausen, K. W., Giannotti, F., Pozdnoukhov, A., Bazzani, A., Wachowicz, M., Ouzounis, G., and Portugali, Y. (2012). Smart cities of the future. *The European Physical Journal Special Topics*, 214(1):481–518.

[Bohn et al., 2011] Bohn, R. B., Messina, J., Liu, F., Tong, J., and Mao, J. (2011). Nist cloud computing reference architecture. In *2011 IEEE World Congress on Services*, pages 594–596. IEEE.

[De Donno et al., 2019] De Donno, M., Tange, K., and Dragoni, N. (2019). Foundations and evolution of modern computing paradigms: Cloud, iot, edge, and fog. *Ieee Access*, 7:150936–150948.

[Dey et al., 2012a] Dey, A. S., Nath, B. J., and Nath, C. A. (2012a). A new technique to hide encrypted data in qr codes (tm). In *Proceedings on the International Conference on Internet Computing (ICOMP)*, page 1. The Steering Committee of The World Congress in Computer Science, Computer . . . .

[Dey, 2012] Dey, S. (2012). Sd-eqr: A new technique to use qr codestm in cryptography. *arXiv preprint arXiv:1205.4829*.

[Dey, 2013] Dey, S. (2013). New generation of digital academic-transcripts using encrypted qr code™: Use of encrypted qr code™ in mark-sheets (academic transcripts). In *2013 International Mutli-Conference on Automation, Computing, Communication, Control and Compressed Sensing (iMac4s)*, pages 313–317. IEEE.

[Dey, 2018a] Dey, S. (2018a). A proof of work: Securing majority-attack in blockchain using machine learning and algorithmic game theory. *International Journal of Wireless and Microwave Technologies*.

[Dey, 2018b] Dey, S. (2018b). Securing majority-attack in blockchain using machine learning and algorithmic game theory: A proof of work. In *2018 10th computer science and electronic engineering (CEEC)*, pages 7–10. IEEE.

[Dey et al., 2013] Dey, S., Agarwal, S., and Nath, A. (2013). Confidential encrypted data hiding and retrieval using qr authentication system. In *2013 International Conference on Communication Systems and Network Technologies*, pages 512–517. IEEE.

[Dey et al., 2019a] Dey, S. et al. (2019a). Edgecoolingmode: An agent based thermal management mechanism for dvfs enabled heterogeneous mpsocs. In *VLSI Design and 18th International Conference on Embedded Systems, 2019. 32nd International Conference on*. IEEE.

[Dey et al., 2020a] Dey, S. et al. (2020a). User interaction aware reinforcement learning for power and thermal efficiency of cpu-gpu mobile mpsocs. In *2020 DATE*. IEEE.

[Dey et al., 2012b] Dey, S., Mondal, K., Nath, J., and Nath, A. (2012b). Advanced steganography algorithm using randomized intermediate qr host embedded with any encrypted secret message: Asa_qr algorithm. *International Journal of Modern Education & Computer Science*, 4(6).

[Dey et al., 2021] Dey, S., Saha, S., Singh, A. K., and McDonald-Maier, K. (2021). Food-sqrblock: Digitizing food production and the supply chain with blockchain and qr code in the cloud. *Sustainability*, 13(6):3486.

[Dey et al., 2022] Dey, S., Saha, S., Singh, A. K., and McDonald-Maier, K. (2022). Smart-noshwaste: Using blockchain, machine learning, cloud computing and qr code to reduce food waste in decentralized web 3.0 enabled smart cities. *Smart Cities*, 5(1):162–176.

[Dey et al., 2019b] Dey, S., Singh, A. K., Prasad, D. K., and Mcdonald-Maier, K. D. (2019b). Socodecnn: Program source code for visual cnn classification using computer vision methodology. *IEEE Access*, 7:157158–157172.

[Dey et al., 2020b] Dey, S., Singh, A. K., Prasad, D. K., and Mcdonald-Maier, K. D. (2020b). Temporal motionless analysis of video using cnn in mpsoc. In *2020 31st IEEE International Conference on Application-specific Systems, Architectures and Processors (ASAP 2020)*. IEEE.

[Drobnik, 2015] Drobnik, O. (2015). *Barcodes with iOS: Bringing together the digital and physical worlds*. Manning.

[El Naqa and Murphy, 2015] El Naqa, I. and Murphy, M. J. (2015). What is machine learning? In *machine learning in radiation oncology*, pages 3–11. Springer.

[Gentleman and Carey, 2008] Gentleman, R. and Carey, V. J. (2008). Unsupervised machine learning. In *Bioconductor case studies*, pages 137–157. Springer.

[Goertzel and Pennachin, 2007] Goertzel, B. and Pennachin, C. (2007). *Artificial general intelligence*, volume 2. Springer.

[Gu et al., 2016] Gu, S., Lillicrap, T., Sutskever, I., and Levine, S. (2016). Continuous deep q-learning with model-based acceleration. In *International conference on machine learning*, pages 2829–2838. PMLR.

[Hakak et al., 2020] Hakak, S., Khan, W. Z., Gilkar, G. A., Imran, M., and Guizani, N. (2020). Securing smart cities through blockchain technology: Architecture, requirements, and challenges. *IEEE Network*, 34(1):8–14.

[Huang et al., 2020] Huang, P.-C., Chang, C.-C., Li, Y.-H., and Liu, Y. (2020). Efficient qr code secret embedding mechanism based on hamming code. *IEEE Access*, 8:86706–86714.

[Irving and Holden, 2016] Irving, G. and Holden, J. (2016). How blockchain-timestamped protocols could improve the trustworthiness of medical science. *F1000Research*, 5.

[Kaelbling et al., 1996] Kaelbling, L. P., Littman, M. L., and Moore, A. W. (1996). Reinforcement learning: A survey. *Journal of artificial intelligence research*, 4:237–285.

[Kamble et al., 2020] Kamble, S. S., Gunasekaran, A., and Sharma, R. (2020). Modeling the blockchain enabled traceability in agriculture supply chain. *International Journal of Information Management*, 52:101967.

[Krishnan and Gonzalez, 2015] Krishnan, S. and Gonzalez, J. L. U. (2015). *Building your next big thing with google cloud platform: A guide for developers and enterprise architects*. Springer.

[Lin, 2016] Lin, P.-Y. (2016). Distributed secret sharing approach with cheater prevention based on qr code. *IEEE Transactions on Industrial Informatics*, 12(1):384–392.

[Marin et al., 2021] Marin, M.-P., Marin, I., and Vidu, L. (2021). Learning about the reduction of food waste using blockchain technology. *arXiv preprint arXiv:2101.02026*.

[Mitchell, 1997] Mitchell, T. M. (1997). Does machine learning really work? *AI magazine*, 18(3):11–11.

[Papargyropoulou et al., 2014] Papargyropoulou, E., Lozano, R., Steinberger, J. K., Wright, N., and bin Ujang, Z. (2014). The food waste hierarchy as a framework for the management of food surplus and food waste. *Journal of cleaner production*, 76:106–115.

[Peris-Ortiz et al., 2017] Peris-Ortiz, M., Bennett, D. R., and Yábar, D. P.-B. (2017). Sustainable smart cities. *Innovation, Technology, and Knowledge Management. Cham: Springer International Publishing Switzerland*.

[Qi and Tao, 2019] Qi, Q. and Tao, F. (2019). A smart manufacturing service system based on edge computing, fog computing, and cloud computing. *IEEE Access*, 7:86769–86777.

[Ragnedda and Destefanis, 2019] Ragnedda, M. and Destefanis, G. (2019). *Blockchain and web 3.0: social, economic, and technological challenges*. Routledge.

[Schanes et al., 2018] Schanes, K., Dobernig, K., and Gözet, B. (2018). Food waste matters-a systematic review of household food waste practices and their policy implications. *Journal of cleaner production*, 182:978–991.

[Singh et al., 2016] Singh, A., Thakur, N., and Sharma, A. (2016). A review of supervised machine learning algorithms. In *2016 3rd International Conference on Computing for Sustainable Global Development (INDIACom)*, pages 1310–1315. Ieee.

[Sutton and Barto, 2018] Sutton, R. S. and Barto, A. G. (2018). *Reinforcement learning: An introduction.* MIT press.

[Teigiserova et al., 2020] Teigiserova, D. A., Hamelin, L., and Thomsen, M. (2020). Towards transparent valorization of food surplus, waste and loss: Clarifying definitions, food waste hierarchy, and role in the circular economy. *Science of The Total Environment*, 706:136033.

[Tian, 2016] Tian, F. (2016). An agri-food supply chain traceability system for china based on rfid & blockchain technology. In *2016 13th international conference on service systems and service management (ICSSSM)*, pages 1–6. IEEE.

[Watkins and Dayan, 1992] Watkins, C. J. and Dayan, P. (1992). Q-learning. *Machine learning*, 8(3-4):279–292.

[Winston, 1992] Winston, P. H. (1992). *Artificial intelligence.* Addison-Wesley Longman Publishing Co., Inc.

[Yiannas, 2018] Yiannas, F. (2018). A new era of food transparency powered by blockchain. *Innovations: Technology, Governance, Globalization*, 12(1-2):46–56.

[Zhao et al., 2019] Zhao, G., Liu, S., Lopez, C., Lu, H., Elgueta, S., Chen, H., and Boshkoska, B. M. (2019). Blockchain technology in agri-food value chain management: A synthesis of applications, challenges and future research directions. *Computers in Industry*, 109:83–99.